BALSALL HEATH
A HISTORY

VALERIE M. HART

BREWIN BOOKS

BREWIN BOOKS
19 Enfield Ind. Estate,
Redditch,
Worcestershire,
B97 6BY
www.brewinbooks.com

First published by Brewin Books 1992

Reprinted February 1993
Reprinted November 1997
Reprinted May 2008
Reprinted with revisions and additional material April 2024

ISBN: 978-1-85858-767-7

British Library Cataloguing in Publication Data.
A Catalogue record for this book is available from the British Library.

Printed and bound in Great Britain
by Halstan & Co. Ltd.

Contents

Maps and Plans

Acknowledgements

Many thanks to all who have made this publication possible, especially Jacqueline Ure who shared the research work, Mick Turner for all his photography and Anita Halliday for her help and support. Thanks also to Patrick Baird and the staff of the Birmingham Central Library Local Studies Department; Stephen Price, formerly of the Birmingham Museum and Art Gallery and St. Paul's Project, Balsall Heath.

Photographs and illustrations have come from many sources, but principally from the Local Studies Department as above, John Marks, the Birmingham Museum and Art Gallery, John Whybrow Ltd, J. H. Butchers, Rylands, C. H. Bradbury's, Birmingham City Planning Department, Pickwick Athletic Club, the Jones family, Mr Mullis, Sheila Fowler, Mr Baker, St. Paul's Church, Paul Cadbury and St. Paul's Project "Heathan Enterprises".

Finally, my thanks to all the present and past residents of Balsall Heath who have brought it all to life through their memories, and particularly to Nell Wilkins, Bernard Jackson and Mary Bramwell of the Balsall Heath Local History Society.

In Memory of
Jim Fitzpatrick

This book is dedicated to the memory of Jim Fitzpatrick, a fine local historian, who contributed much energy and expertise to this book's republishing.

A Short Bibliography

Victoria County History, Vols 1 and 7
A History of Birmingham, Vol 1 by Gill, Vol 2 by Asa Briggs
The Making of Birmingham by A. Dent
Victorian Birmingham by Victor Skipp
Our Birmingham published by Cadbury's, 1943
Bygone Birmingham by Dyke Wilkinson
Birmingham on Old Postcards by John Marks
History of Moseley by Alison Fairn
Richard Cadbury by Helen Alexander
A Short Review of Birmingham Tramways by Hardy and Jacques
Showell's Dictionary of Birmingham, 1885
Local Studies in Balsall Heath and Highgate ⎫
Bygone Balsall Heath ⎭ Morris Jones
Some Records of an Old House by Simcox
Father Pollock and His Brother by J. S. Pollock
Vaughton's Hole – 125 Years in it by J. S. Pollock
Writing it Down Before it's all Gone ⎫
Memories of Balsall Heath and Highgate ⎭ ed. by Alan Mahar

Sketch Map of the Balsall Heath Area c.1780 by Val Hart: Derived from contemporary maps and information.

Chapter 1
The 18th Century

For centuries, Birmingham was a small town of little importance but in the 18th century it started to grow rapidly. It was a town where people were free to pursue a trade unrestricted by ancient craft guilds or traditions. It attracted men of initiative, endeavour and enterprise such as Boulton and Watt, as well as a myriad of small manufacturers. Its remarkable development at this time is reflected in its population growth from 15,000 in 1700 to 70,000 in 1800.

This then was the spur to the development of Balsall Heath, an area lying on the south west flank of the mushrooming town. Such an increasing population had to be fed and the main route from the productive Vale of Evesham to the Birmingham market, lay across the Heath. By mid-century as many as 80 packhorses a day were trudging their way across the muddy heathland to Birmingham.[1] Such pressure of use demanded an improved road and this was achieved in 1767 when a Turnpike Trust was established complete with toll gates at Kyrwicks Lane at one end of the Heath, and Edgbaston Lane at the other. The way was paved for development.

Balsall Heath was at that time a small community, an insignificant corner of King's Norton Parish. The 1782 Rate Book lists only 12 occupiers of houses on the Heath, and the land enclosed in 1774 was divided among a mere handful of people. The area was quite prosperous, however. Travellers could pause for refreshment at various coaching inns, such as The Woodman on Highgate Road, or The Angel on Stratford Road which is still there but now a restaurant.

Other forms of entertainment for weary town dwellers were also available locally. For example, Vaughton's Hole on the River Rea, was apparently the ideal spot for a rural dip [for location see map]. In 1745 an advertisement appeared in *Aris's Gazette*, one of the Birmingham newspapers, for the return of a silver pocket watch taken from a gentleman's pocket while he was bathing. There was a valuable reward of "One guinea, and no questions asked."

The Angel Inn c.1870.

Near Vaughton's Hole.

2

The Moseley Road, near Highgate, also offered entertainment briefly in 1778 when a theatre opened there. It offered comic interludes, farces and opera. Unfortunately, it burnt to the ground as a result of arson. Apparently many of the townspeople found it "Ungodly and immoral."

MOSELEY THEATRE, Moseley Road, in the parish of Aston :-

August 18, 1778.

"WHEREAS on Thursday Night last, the Concert Booth, somewhat beyond the Plough and Harrow, on the Moseley Road, erected for Theatrical Amusements, was in a rapid Manner entirely burnt down to Ground, together with all the Scenery, and a Part of the Company's Cloaths. And whereas, from various Circumstances, a strong Suspicion arises, that the said Booth was wilfully set on Fire. NOTICE is hereby given, that if any one can give such Information, as may lead to an Apprehension of the Person or Persons who perpetrated the said Act, shall, on Conviction, receive Ten Guineas from Mr. Godry, Builder, ~ New Hall Hill, Birmingham." ·X·

Extracts from Everson's History of Balsall Heath and Moseley.

The tannery bell, dated 1749. Now in St. Cyprian's Church, Hay Mills.

3

Meanwhile the local inhabitants were hard at work. There was a substantial tannery on the Moseley Road from the 1740s which thrived in the hands of the Edwards and Homer family for many generations.[2] By 1802 the premises included a large tan yard, with barns and store rooms, as well as a mansion house and 70 acres of rich arable land.[3] A sale notice of 1834 remarked: "The situation is inferior to none in the kingdom for the purchase of hides and bark, and the never failing supply of water."[4] It stood on the site of the present Lime Grove.[5]

Edgbaston Mill.

The watermills on the River Rea were also successful enterprises, changing their use flexibly according to need. By the 1780s the Edgbaston mill had turned away from milling corn to the rolling of metal. So too, had the Speedwell Mill, further down the river.[6]

However, most of the land in Balsall Heath was probably taken up with farming. Local farms in the 18th century advertised cattle, pasture land, crops and even apparently made cheese. A remnant of one local farm still survives; Stratford House on the Moseley Road, originally built in 1601. This was held by the Simcox family from 1696 to 1926.

A corner of the house from Some records of an old house *by Simcox 1896.*

John Walford Simcox and his mother c.1870.

Stratford House, Highgate, Birmingham, 1601.

Originally the estate comprised about 20 acres, but it was cut in two by the railway in 1838 and developed for housing in the second half of the 19th century.

Another farm called "Longmoors" was held by Dr. John Cox, who was chaplain of Deritend for 40 years. The name of it was derived from "Long Marsh" which seems likely since its land stretched along the Rea and was undoubtedly subject to flooding. The name is recorded as early as 1608 and in 1798 the farmhouse was described as "the white cottage just beyond Vaughton's Hole."[7] Longmoors was not sold off until 1869[8] and meanwhile the Cox family had a significant part to play in Balsall Heath. Edward Townsend Cox, the prominent surgeon, lived in the area from 1830 till his death at the age of 93, in 1863.

Although the population of Balsall Heath was sparse at the end of the 18th century, those who lived there were anxious about the crime rate. The maintenance of law and order was still the responsibility of King's Norton Parish authorities but arrangements for dealing with crime were not very satisfactory. In 1778, a group of residents from Balsall Heath and Moseley together formed "The Association for the Prosecution of Felons". The members of this association all contributed money for the payment of rewards to persons whose information led to the capture of offenders. A £5 reward was paid for a housebreaker or stealer of animals; one guinea for those destroying orchards, gardens or fish ponds, clothes and grounds; and 10/6 for those stealing gate fittings, plough irons and harrow teeth.[9] Obviously Balsall Heath and Moseley were still very rural in nature.

By 1801 the rewards had risen. Six guineas were now offered for a person convicted of a capital offence, four guineas for a transportation crime and two guineas for lesser misdeeds. Toll gate keepers were especially mentioned. They were to receive a one guinea reward for any "horse stealer, highway robber or any other person who shall have stolen cattle or sheep, or any housebreaker."[10]

The Association was prepared to combat crime but they can hardly have envisaged the outburst of lawlessness during the extraordinary riots which shook Birmingham for several days in 1791.

They were sparked off by a banquet held at Dingley's Hotel in town, on July 14th to celebrate the anniversary of the French Revolution, most of the guests being both radical in their sympathies and non-conformist in their religion. The occasion aroused great hostility among some Birmingham people who had been alarmed and distressed by the turmoil in France. They saw the banqueters as traitors to Church and King, and succeeded in gathering a large, angry mob who stormed the hotel, breaking down doors and windows and damaging furniture. Dr. Joseph Priestley was one of the main targets of the rioters. He was a scientist, a radical and the minister of the Unitarian Chapel in New Meeting Street, which was burnt to the ground by the rioters. Not content with this, the mob streamed out of Birmingham towards Balsall Heath because Priestley's house, Fair Hill, stood near the site of the present Larches Green.

Here too, the building was set on fire, his valuable library of books and his laboratories destroyed. After the ransack of the wine cellars, however, some of the rioters became very drunk and lost their lives. One was killed by falling masonry while seven others were too intoxicated to escape the fire. Priestley himself fled to London, never to return. A

Priestley's House Fair Hill, 1891.

plaque in Priestley Road commemorates the site of his house, where he lived from 1784 until it was burnt down in 1791.

Hobson's School was another target in Balsall Heath attacked by the rioters. In 1788 the Reverend John Hobson, a Protestant Dissenting Minister, set up a private school for eight young gentlemen, in a large house on the Heath. It had only been open for two and a half years when the rioters, in July 1791, surged out of town along the turnpike road to Moseley and, finding the school in their path, attacked it, merely because Hobson was a Dissenter. He escaped in disguise with his family when he heard the mob approaching and an eye-witness reported: "About twelve o'clock that day poor Mrs Hobson came, such a picture of fatigue and distress as I never saw before – a delicate little woman without hat or cloak, in her nightcap with one child in one arm and a large bundle under the other; she came in almost breathless, threw herself on a chair and nearly fainted".[11] Another comment at the time was, "As riches could not save a man, neither could property. The mob next fell upon a poor but sensible presbyterian parson, the Reverend John Hobson of Balsall Heath, and burnt his all". A sad auction sale was held in November of that year of the goods saved from the fire. It included 12 excellent fine feather beds and bedding, so clearly the boarders were given comfortable quarters![12]

Balsall Heath in 1790 was then a small rural area but already the sounds of industry and bustling activity could be heard across the fields of Highgate. Birmingham was growing fast and approaching closer.

1.   V.C.H. Vol 1.
2.   BRL: 374776 Indenture re Tannery 1741.
3.   Title deeds of Richard Tariton. BRL: 380086. DV. 395.
4.   BRL: Everson's chronological History of King's Heath, Moseley and Balsall Heath. 13 Vols. May 1833.
5.   Edwards Estate Map. July 1833. BRL: 383129.
6.   Aris's Gazette. May 30 1785.
7.   Ibid. Aug. 24 1829.
8.   Everson. June 1869.
9.   Ibid. Feb. 1778.
10. Bickley. Birmingham Broadsides and news cuttings.
11. Aris's Gazette. July 1791.
12. Ibid. July 1791.

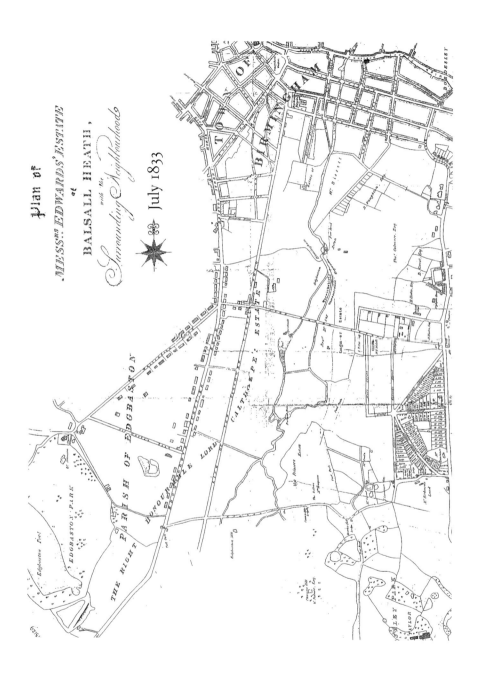

Plan of
MESS.ᴿˢ EDWARDS' ESTATE
at
BALSALL HEATH,
with the
Surrounding Neighbourhood
☆ July 1833

Chapter 2

A Genteel Neighbourhood
c.1790 – 1830

In the 40 years following the riots, Balsall Heath and neighbouring Highgate slowly acquired more inhabitants, mostly of a rather well-to-do kind. By the 1790s a ribbon of substantial residences for the successful was threading its way along the main road at Highgate, towards Balsall Heath.[1] Some of these are still here today.

Houses opposite Highgate Park, on the Moseley Road.

These were no hastily constructed quarters for the down-trodden workers of the Industrial Revolution, but rather gracious and impressive houses for wealthy manufacturers, seeking to distance themselves and their families from the smoky hub of their business world. Often these self-made men had started out in the centre of Birmingham with a workshop in the backyard of their houses. As trade expanded, the whole garden was gradually taken up, and finally the house itself. At this point they stepped smartly several rungs up the social ladder and moved to a fashionable house in the rural, and cheaper, suburbs where they could now afford to live in style, with servants, expensive furniture, garden and probably a carriage and horses.

S.E. aspect of Birmingham. c.1830.

This was a period, then, when Balsall Heath was dominated by a number of quite large houses, some set in their own "pleasure grounds". Typical of this new type of residence was a house advertised for tenancy in 1801: "2 parlours, a kitchen, nine lodging rooms, a brewhouse, with a stable, large garden walled around, well-planted with choice fruit trees, with about an acre of land, situated at Balsall Heath. The situation is desirable, being healthy and in a genteel neighbourhood".[2]

Unfortunately Stratford House is the only one of these earlier residences to survive today. Fair Hill fell to the rioters in 1791 but The

Larches nearby was not so extensively damaged. This was occupied in 1799 by Dr. William Withering, famous for his discovery of digitalis in foxgloves as a treatment for heart disease. He moved here from Edgbaston in search of purer air and level fields, but unfortunately died almost at once![3] The house was finally demolished in 1874 to make way for new streets of housing at "Larches Green".

Another imposing mansion was Highgate House which stood in about 22 acres of land near the site of the present day traffic lights at Highgate Road.[4] It was built towards the end of the 18th century and its attractive features included "a stone flagged entrance hall with stone staircase, eight lodging rooms, water closet, butler's and china pantries, excellent cellars, productive gardens, plantations, lawns, carriage houses and stables".[5] Henry Haden, a button manufacturer, lived here with his wife Ann from about 1791 to 1837.[6] He and his wife are both buried at Moseley and there is an interesting plaque to their memory in St. Mary's Church.

Another house from earlier times called "Ball's House" stood in Edgbaston Lane between Moseley Road and Mary Street.

Ball's House. Photo of watercolour in the museum, by Warren Blackham.

Also at this end of the Heath stood Balsall Heath House dating from the mid-18th century and owned by the Balden family who were closely involved in the firm now known as Avery's, makers of weighing machines. In 1816 when Joseph Balden, senior, died, the estate was valued at £3,500, a lot of money in those days. Unfortunately his 18-year -old son, Joseph, was a rather wild young man who indulged in heavy drinking, horse racing and amusements of all kinds. His excesses led him to confinement in an asylum at Henley-in-Arden in 1816, where he stayed for many years.[7] Meanwhile the house was let to a Mr and Mrs French who opened a preparatory school for 25 young gentlemen, aged 4-10 years.[8] The house and estate remained at the centre of long and bitter legal battles, however, as Joseph's younger brother, Samuel, never accepted the settlements made. Matters came to a head when Joseph died in 1843, and the house was put in the hands of temporary caretakers. On two occasions, Samuel broke into the house with a gang, and did considerable damage![9]

The tannery on the Heath has already been mentioned. It was a large and well-established enterprise in these years and included substantial gentlemanly living accommodation.

After Henry Homer died, his widow Betty moved out of the house at the tannery in 1808, to occupy a separate establishment further along

Mr Homer's House, Balsall Heath, Watercolour by S. Wright, 1799.
The tannery appears to be behind the house.

14

Painting of Mrs Homer's residence, opposite Balsall Heath Road, by artist Paul Braddon c.1840.

Workers at the Yardley Tannery c.1900.

the Moseley Road.[10] One of her sons Avery Edwards Homer, continued to run the business till it finally closed in 1833.[11]

His brother, Henry, married a girl called Ann Chambers from Yardley and it was there that they settled and founded a new tannery which survived till 1966, and was one of the last traditional oak bark tanneries in the country.

Oakfield House, another of these large houses, apparently had rural surroundings. It was built by Thomas Cooke, a successful Birmingham brassfounder, who lived there with his wife Ann. Its grounds included a piggery, fish ponds, farm buildings and also six acres of pasture land "thickly studded with full grown majestic oaks".[12] In 1828 when his wife died, Thomas Cooke divided up the land and three other large residences were built there, approached by a carriage road from Edgbaston Lane. These were also rather grand places. Oak House even had its own "fountain with large temple" and "a vinery".[13]

This was Balsall Heath in the late 1820s; respectable, genteel and rural, untouched as yet by large-scale development of either housing or industry. However everything was on the brink of change.

1. Map. BRL: 383129.
2. *Everson.* Aug. 1801.
3. *A Memoir of the Life, Character and Writings of William Withering.* Pub. 1822. BRL: 2429.
4. Highgate House was later also called Balsall Heath House. Map. BRL: 383129.
5. *Everson.* May 1838.
6. *Everson's 1896 Directory and Memorial in Church of St. Mary's,* Moseley.
7. *Balden Family and Estate. A New Procedure in Conveyancing.* 1835. BRL: 62755.
8. *Everson.* July 29 1816.
9. a) *Balsall Heath Riot.* Pub. 1847. BRL: 60389.
   b) Pamphlet. BRL: 60388. 1845.
   c) Lee Crowder deeds. 1252 and 1253.
10. *Everson* March 1808.
11. Ibid., May 1832.
12. Ibid., Feb. 1828.
13. Ibid., Sept. 1870.

Chapter 3

Exceedingly Eligible for Villa Residences
c.1829 – 1840

August 10th 1829, was an important milestone in Balsall Heath's history. On that day three of the owners of estates lying between the Moseley Road and the Pershore Road agreed to form a new highway to link these two turnpike roads together. It was to cost the enormous sum of £1,000 and included a bridge over the River Rea.[1] So Balsall Heath Road was built with a crossing place for carriages, the next one being at Edgbaston Lane. By 1829 Birmingham was growing faster than ever and Edgbaston had already become established as a fashionable suburb. The time was ripe for new housing development. First of the estates to be sold off was that of William Moore of Staffordshire who went

View of Birmingham from Highgate c.1840.

bankrupt in 1829.[2] The sales particulars described his land as "exceedingly eligible for villa residences. The commanding nature of the situation, affording extensive prospects over a rich and beautiful country, place them on a par with the most enviable of the Edgbaston retreats".[3] However, the building plots were of a modest size and a network of roads was laid out that was not particularly spacious. These "villa" residences were clearly not going to rival those of Edgbaston!

Meanwhile important developments were taking place in Highgate, as both housing and industry advanced in close proximity to each other, pressing outwards from Birmingham towards Balsall Heath. Typical of this period was the brassfounding factory of Samuel Heath's, established in the new Leopold Street in 1830. It is still there today, still in the Heath family after five generations, and still producing the fine quality brassware for which it became renowned. A magnificent brass clock was their contribution to the Great Exhibition in 1851. Housing sprang up around this factory as the firm provided homes for its employees.

Samuel Heath and Sons, Leopold Street, 1988.

A smaller replica of Heath's brassware clock.

Back in Balsall Heath itself, the lure of a quick profit was undoubtedly the spur to further development. The sale of the estate of the Rev. Vincent Edwards, from 1833 onwards, offered a golden opportunity. Roads were laid out carefully and named after members of the family. The sale notices reverberated with rolling phrases describing the amazing attraction of the land on offer: "highly valuable and truly picturesque"... "the universally acknowledged beauty of the situation"... "views of the Rea Valley... With finely wooded, rich and undulating country". Nor were these the only advantages to be gained. Rates were low as Balsall Heath was part of the rural parish of King's Norton. Possibly even more enticing was the chance to buy a freehold plot of land which would entitle its owner to a county vote for East Worcester.[4]

Housing in Mary Street.

Mary Street, 1970.

The profit motive was quite explicit in the intensive sales campaign, too. In 1835, an auction notice boasted "it is presumed speculators will be alive to this sale, purchasers having realised from the re-sale of parts bought at former auctions, within the space of 12 months from 50% to 100% profit".[5]

However, the profits were derived mainly from increasing land values in the new and promising suburb, rather than from the mass development of housing. Plots were sold individually and houses built either singly or a few at a time, some of them for owner occupiers. Sizes and styles varied enormously but the generally slow pace is shown by the 1841 census when there were still only nine houses in Tindal Street and 11 in Mary Street. There were small workshops, too, and also in Vincent Street in 1839 a Methodist Chapel, the first religious institution in the area, now sadly demolished.

Meanwhile, other owners of land in the area were watching closely, wondering whether or not to sell up at this point. The Haden's land had already come on the market in 1837 and Belgrave Road was cut through in 1838.

There were now plans for the development of land on the east side of the Moseley Road too. However, a startlingly modern invention was due to arrive shortly.

February 1837 saw the beginning of the Birmingham to Gloucester railway line, running through Balsall Heath.[6] Obviously to some inhabitants, this represented progress! At last there would be a rapid and effective means of communication with Birmingham for both goods and passengers. What a bonus both for new industry and housing!

On the other hand, to some landowners the railway posed a considerable threat. Humphrey Pountney of Monyhull Hall, for example, owned land in the area of the present Brighton Road. He protested furiously: "an embankment of this kind will be a serious injury for its unseemliness and its shading of the land".[7] One can understand his point of view. Suddenly his 12 acres were to be dominated by a 16ft high embankment cutting off access to the main road. Worse still, shrieking trains would hurtle past his peaceful building plots! He received meagre compensation and the railway company built bridges (which were always too narrow), but his hopes of speedy cash profits were dashed.

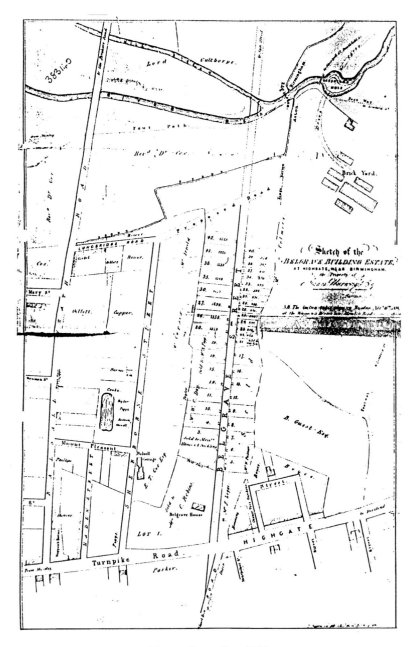

Belgrave Estate Plan, 1838.

The case ran through the courts and the railway won. Trains steamed across Balsall Heath from the 1840s and effectively retarded the development of building land on this side of the Moseley Road for the following 20 years. For the rest of Balsall Heath, however, the railway was a great leap forward. Camp Hill Station opened in December 1840, approximately on the site of the Highgate Road traffic lights. From here it was a mere $2^{1}/_{2}$ hours to Gloucester, or one could speedily travel to Birmingham and from there to Liverpool, Manchester, or even London. Balsall Heath had suddenly become part of a much bigger world!

Entrance to Camp Hill Station on the Moseley Road.

1. *Everson.* Aug. 1829.
2. *Everson's Directory* 1896.
3. *Everson.* Aug. 24 1829.
4. Ibid., July 1833, Nov. and June 1835.
5. Ibid., Aug. 1835.
6. Ibid., Feb. 1837.
7. Ibid., April 1837.

The Old Ship Inn, Camp Hill, c. late 1800s.

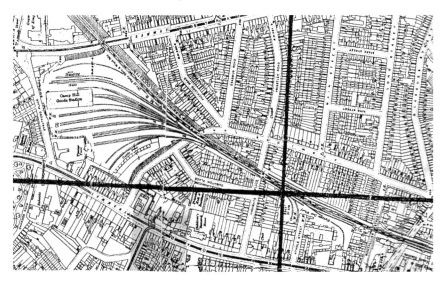

Part of the 1890 O.S. Map showing the extent of Camp Hill Station and Goods Yard.

Chapter 4
Vigorous Development
c.1840 – 1862

The middle years of the 19th century saw the infant Balsall Heath struggle through its first phases of development and begin to establish itself. Links with Birmingham were strengthened by the opening of the railway station and in 1846 another form of public transport made its appearance; the horse-drawn omnibus, which plied the Moseley Road about 6 times a day on weekdays. This was an important and useful service but comfort had a very low priority. The inside was packed with straw almost as high as the seats while upstairs passengers ascended a vertical ladder to perch on the "knifeboard" seats with their legs dangling over the side. Precarious though this was, the chief complaint of passengers was not the danger, or the weather, but overcrowding.[1]

Horse bus on Stratford Road c.1912. Main Street can be seen to the right in the background, Farm Road to the left.

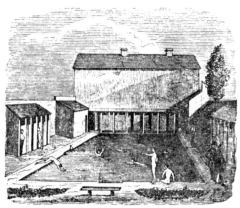

BALSALL HEATH

BATHS,

PROPRIETOR,

JOHN SMITH,

Who begs most respectfully to call the attention of the Gentry and Public in general to his newly erected Bathing Establishment; the Proprietor having studied the comfort and convenience of persons bathing has spared no expense in fitting up the Baths in the best of style; they are supplied with a continual flow of soft Spring Water; are delightfully situated in George street, Balsall Heath, a most commanding and, at the same time, a retired position, about twenty minutes walk from the centre of the Town.

Tickets for the Season, 10s. 6d.   Private Bath, 1s.   Single Bath, 6d.

Also to be Sold valuable Freehold Land adjoining the Baths, in lots of 11 or 22 yards frontage, apply as above, or at the Globe, Great Barr-street.

From Wrightsons Directory, 1847.

Balsall Heath by now had several attractions of its own to draw visitors from Birmingham. One of these was the private swimming baths in George Street, which opened in 1846. When the Edwards Estate was sold off, several plots were purchased by an enterprising individual called John Smith who then exploited the constant supply of natural spring water on the land. His handsome bathing establishment catered for the new wave of public enthusiasm for swimming in the 1840s. There was a large pool, about 100ft by 50ft and two or three private baths as well. It was Birmingham's first open-air swimming pool, and was available to the public only in the summer season. Admission charges of 6d and 1/- suggest that the baths were designed for the leisured classes and an advertisement also offered "stabling and other conveniences for the accommodation of gentlemen attending in carriages or on horseback." The baths were chiefly provided for men only, and it seems that bathing costumes were not worn. The baths flourished for about the next 30 years.[2]

Another attraction was provided by the tea gardens of the Orange Tree Tavern on the Moseley Road, near Highgate Square. In the 1850s the townspeople of Birmingham could stroll out on a summer evening along the Rea Valley, over the river by stepping stones and cross the fields to the Orange Tree. "Here they could indulge in a game of bowls, partake of a brew of tea, or of a stronger beverage for which home-brew the Orange Tree was famous; and sitting at ease in the arbours and alcoves, watch the sun sink behind the spires and chimneys of the town across the valley".[3]

Orange Tree Tavern, Moseley Road, 1860.

There was more to life than leisure pursuits, however. Mixed among the ever-increasing houses were a number of workshops and small factories. An example dating from 1849 was Watton and Sellers

Imperial Ropery in Mary Street, which had a rope walk stretching from Mary Street to Wenman Street.[4] This was an area where the ropes were laid out, and remained in use until 1908.

The Birmingham City Museum has an interesting machine used by this firm for balling string.

Balls of twine or cord could be wound to the desired weight by counting the number of turns of the handle.

28

Meanwhile, the inhabitants of Balsall Heath were ready to turn their minds to higher things. About 1850, a young clergyman called Rev. Benison came to Balsall Heath to look for a house for his relations. He found the area very appealing. Open fields lay behind the railway towards Ladypool Lane while the River Rea, in the other direction was still a sparkling stream lined with berry bushes. The clergyman, who later became the first incumbent of the parish, looked around, and felt that only one thing was missing – a church.[5]

He was not alone in his views. In May 1850 seven gentlemen met in Edward Townsend Cox's house, Balsall Cottage, to discuss ways and means of erecting a church. This was followed by a public meeting in the Waggon and Horses on the Moseley Road before building work finally started in 1852.[6] St. Paul's Church was consecrated amid a blaze of publicity the following year, with seats for 1,111 people of which 500 were allocated to the congregation by name. It immediately became a popular and fashionable focal point for Balsall Heath and exerted a considerable influence.

St. Paul's Church, 1906.

The new parishioners were not content to sit back at this point, however. They perceived an urgent need for educational provision for the parish children and quickly set about establishing two church schools. The first of these opened in Vincent Street in 1857 and comprised three classrooms, one each for boys, girls and infants, as well as a house for the schoolmaster and schoolmistress.[7] Ladypool Lane School which followed in 1858,[8] also provided staff accommodation but seems to have been built on a smaller budget. Here the boys and girls departments were divided only by a curtain.[9] By 1853, Balsall Heath had two religious buildings: the small Methodist chapel in Vincent Street and the imposing St. Paul's Church in Moseley Road. Other initiatives were also being taken, however, including the establishment of the charming Hope Street Baptist Chapel in 1854.

1. A. G. Jensen. *Birmingham Transport*. BRL: 894899.
2. 1871 Census and Local Board of Health Minutes. Dec. 1877.
3. *Birmingham Weekly Post*. 19-11-21. BRL: 304625.
4. Watton and Sellers' memo heading: Birmingham Museum and Art Gallery.
5. *St. Paul's Church, The First Hundred Years*. 1953 (lent by St. Paul's Church).
6. *Everson*. April 1852.
7. Jan. 1857.
8. *St. Paul's Church. The First Hundred Years*. (as above).
9. Birmingham Institutions. BRL: 388.820.

Chapter 5

A Populous Quarter – The Work of the Local Board of Health c.1862 – 1891

By 1862 the previously rural neighbourhood was giving way to an urban suburb, with a population of an astonishing 10,000,[1] housed in about 10 miles of public streets.[2] The bewildered parish officers of King's Norton were at their wits end. How were they to assess and collect rates from a multitude of new houses, formulate building regulations, pave and name new streets, arrange for disposal of rubbish and so on?[3] At last in 1858 a Local Government Act was passed which allowed locally elected bodies to levy rates for both sanitary and street improvements. So in 1862 the Balsall Heath Local Board of Health was established, with sole responsibility for the management of the district, with the exception of the poor law. A new era of independence had dawned, which was to last till 1891.

Members of the board were unpaid but they quickly appointed four employees, a Surveyor, a Clerk, and an Inspector of Nuisances, who were all paid £60 p.a. and a Collector of Rates who was paid by results – that is, he had a commission of 2% on the money he collected![4]

The task facing them was colossal. Here was a whole new suburb which was developing all around them on a piecemeal and makeshift basis. There was no organised water supply – often many houses shared a pump which drew water directly from underground. There was also no sewage system. Frequently the privies were situated within a few yards of the water pump.[5]

To add to their difficulties, Balsall Heath also combined some of the disadvantages of both town and country. The Inspector of Nuisances frequently reported some of the newly arrived factories and workshops for urban problems such as "emitting noxious fumes" or for too much noise. At the same time, many of the inhabitants felt it their right to keep pigs in the back yard as they had done in the country, and became

PLAN OF THE
URBAN SANITARY DISTRICT
OF
BALSALL HEATH.
IN THE
Parish of Kings Norton + County of Worcester.
PUBLISHED BY ORDER OF THE BOARD, SAM OWEN, C.E., SURVEYOR.

Scale 6 Chains to One Inch.

indignant about the regulations imposed on them. For example, a proposal in 1874 for the removal of all pigs was regarded by a meeting of ratepayers as "oppressive and an infringement of rights".[6] Balsall Heath had its last outbreak of Foot and Mouth Disease in 1882.

This was a time of readjustment for a lot of people. They came mainly from the surrounding countryside in search of new opportunities in town. Now they had the luxury of street lamps, and well-surfaced roads but also they had to adapt to a new situation, where they found themselves living in close proximity to many, many others. Rubbish disposal, for example, in the new terraces of Balsall Heath had to be organised and controlled. Horatio Taylor, the Inspector of Nuisances, was chiefly responsible for the sanitary state of the area and waged a constant war on this problem. As late as 1882 a handbill was published, threatening legal proceedings against those who "indulged in the pernicious practice of throwing refuse out of their houses and shops on to the street".[7]

The Surveyor's job was also demanding but less contentious. He chiefly supervised the construction of new roads and buildings, ensuring they reached the regulated standards. Exterior walls of dwellings had to be 9" thick, rooms 8' high with at least one window.

The board conducted their business at first from the St. Paul's Schools in Vincent Street, but the volume of work made a permanent base a necessity. In 1875 they moved into fine new premises in Lime Grove.

Moseley Road, c.1885, showing the Methodist Church and Local Board sign.

33

Much progress was made in the early years of the board, but the major problems of sewerage and water supply were unfortunately postponed. In 1873 this brought a crisis for the board when there was a sudden typhoid epidemic.

By January 6th 1873, 50 families were affected, a total of 96 cases. More surprisingly, half of these were in Moseley in "the best villa residences". Dr. Ballard, a medical inspector for the Local Government Board in London, was called in and he made his report to an emergency meeting of the Balsall Heath Board on January 11th.[8]

The cause lay in the polluted well of two particular milk sellers who lived in adjoining houses in Balsall Heath. They both supplied milk to Moseley and one of the first people to die of typhoid in the area was a boy who helped one of the milkmen. The milk itself came from a farm in the country a few miles beyond Moseley but it seems that both Balsall Heath milkmen were guilty of mixing the milk with water to increase their profits, and it was the water which caused the infection. The wells at the two dairies were a mere 13ft from the privies and Dr. Ballard thought the death of a visitor there in November had probably originally brought the disease to the district.

Blame for the outbreak was placed firmly on the shoulders of the local board because they had failed to make sure there was a supply of pure water to the district. Dr. Ballard went further, to add that he had inspected a number of wells locally and found "there was not one of them that was not polluted and there was one in which it was said that the water would make excellent manure". He believed that the sewage system was so inadequate in Balsall Heath that all the wells were likely to be polluted.

Immediate action was obviously needed and the board hastily erected standpipes supplying pure town water to the local inhabitants. These stayed in position for six months and handbills were then circulated to the people asking them to apply for a connection to the piped water supply if they wished it. This was a far from satisfactory solution. The board itself refused to pay the cost of piping water into individual houses, and in the majority of cases the cost was too high for either landlords or owner occupiers. Once again, it was a makeshift arrangement and wells continued to be used unless the Inspector of Nuisances found the water unfit.

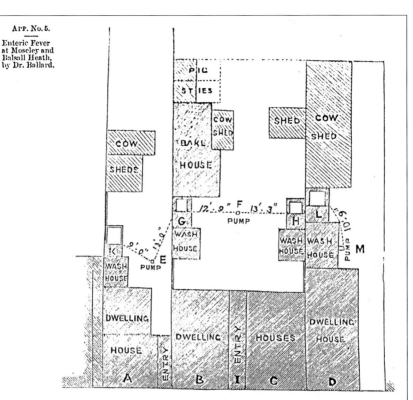

App. No. 5.

Enteric Fever at Moseley and Balsall Heath, by Dr. Ballard.

Scale 22 feet to 1 inch.

App. No. 5.

Enteric Fever at Moseley and Balsall Heath, by Dr. Ballard.

The etiology of the outbreak of enteric fever at Moseley and Balsall Heath may, in my opinion, be thus summed up :—

1. Two wells upon adjoining premises occupied by milk-sellers, became infected early in November with the infectious matter or virus of enteric fever through the soakage from a privy into them of excremental matters containing that matter of infection.

2. Through the medium of water drawn from these wells the milk supplied by these milk-sellers became infected, and many of their regular customers who drank the milk suffered from the disease.

3. The same infected milk having been sold to two other milk purveyors, some of the persons using the milk supplied by these milkmen also suffered in a similar manner.

4. There is no evidence that the disease spread in these districts in any other way than through the consumption of these infected milks.

Extracts from a report by Dr. Ballard (Parliamentary Reports 117. Public Health 1873).

However, a step forward was taken. A Medical Officer for Balsall Heath was at last appointed, under whose guidance vaccination was introduced, especially against smallpox.[9] In spite of its difficulties, Balsall Heath's death rate tended to be consistently lower than that of neighbouring Birmingham.

Meanwhile, the problem of sewage disposal remained. Over-reliance on the River Rea as a means of drainage had caused serious pollution by 1877, and this became the object of a satirical attack in the Birmingham periodical, *The Dart*.

> *"Roll on, thou shallow dirty river – roll!*
> *Ten thousand cats have ended life in thee*
> ....
> ....
> *Improvement marks the town, but its control*
> *Stops at thy shore, it hath done naught for thee*
> *But thou art still neglected murky Rea*
> *For no-one ever speaks or thinks of cleansing thee."*

Until 1882, a series of methods of disposing of sewage were adopted. Firstly there were the ordinary privies which were most common, and which were emptied by the "night soil men". Secondly, drainage tanks were built to prevent pollution of the Spark Brook which ran part of the way along Stoney Lane before turning on its journey towards the Warwickshire Canal. Thirdly, attempts were made to come to some agreement with Birmingham for making junctions with their sewage pipes. In 1876 the board took a major step forward when it agreed to pay for the use of these pipes to convey sewage to Saltley for treatment. The fee was 1/3 per head per year, and 10/- for each water closet in the district. At last in 1882 came the establishment of a complete sewage system in Balsall Heath which had a marked effect on the Rea. Efforts were made to clean it up and in 1891 *The Dart* reported "Water is now a good colour and a nice height. The colder weather and stiff winds have much improved the pike fishing and a few good catches have been made in the deep water by Deritend Bridge."

Meanwhile problems continued on the other side of the Moseley Road as the system proved inadequate and the Spark Brook became increasingly polluted. Residents of Ladypool Lane suffered from frequent floods and the board became increasingly entangled in long and expensive legal disputes both with the Birmingham and Warwick Canal Company and the Kings Norton Sanitary Authority. By 1891 the board had accumulated a debt of £50,000 largely for legal costs! In 1887 *The Dart* commented on the situation with its usual relish: "How long is Noodledom going to reign?... The sewers have been there two years and have been paid for, but the Balsall Heath Board of Noodles can't agree with the Rural Board of Bumbles and the United Drainage Bunglers about some questions of cost. So there is the smell and there are the useless drains!"

In other areas of its work the board was more successful, however. In 1878 it established the first, Balsall Heath Fire Brigade, spending £200 on equipment which included a hose reel, fire escape ladder, jumping sheet, axes and chains. The eight firemen were unpaid and rather inefficient! Improvements were made as time passed. From 1880 firemen were paid a modest fee and by 1891 Balsall Heath could boast a proper fire station and, most wonderful of all, a truly modern steam fire engine.

There was also from 1869, a fine police station in Edward Road, still standing there today. This was not directly under the control of the board but obviously close co-operation was needed as the board's horses were kept in the stables there. Crime statistics are unfortunately not available, but a sample of the work is provided by the local newspaper in 1880. A man was arrested in Mary Street for being "drunk in charge of a horse".

William Bartlett, fireman, in Lime Grove, c.1882.

BALSALL HEATH LOCAL BOARD.

RE QUESTION OF

ANNEXATION

TO

CITY OF BIRMINGHAM.

To the Ratepayers & Property Owners

The Boundaries Sub-Committee of the City Council having proposed terms for the inclusion or absorption within the City area of the District of the Balsall Heath Local Board of Health, the Local Board have decided, before giving an answer to such proposal, to take instructions from the ratepayers and property owners of the district, at a meeting to be specially called for the purpose.

I therefore invite your attendance at such meeting, to be held at the

BOARD SCHOOLS, TINDAL STREET,

BALSALL HEATH,

On Monday Next, the 10th November, inst.,

AT EIGHT P.M.,

for the purpose of passing or rejecting the undermentioned resolution.

J. R. O. TAUNTON,

Chairman of the Local Board.

1891 poster.

Throughout its existence, the board was always at the centre of controversy and elections were hotly contested. Benjamin Tipper, who lived in Tindal Street near his animal food factory, was one of the most outspoken critics and a founder member of the Ratepayers Protection Society. He was elected to the board himself in 1875 to the cry of "Tipper and good footpaths."[10] In 1881, however, his election campaign

Balsall Heath Library, 1910.

based on the board's "Shameless and extravagant expenditure" apparently did not win public support. Other members of the board included successful businessmen like John Bowen, a local builder, and local gentlemen such as John Towers Lawrence.

Was the local board a failure then? In many respects it was not. Proposals made by the Borough of Birmingham for annexation were vigorously rebuffed in 1867, 1884 and 1887 partly out of local pride and partly because Balsall Heath rates were always substantially lower than those of Birmingham! However there were obvious difficulties in trying to run a small district like Balsall Heath on the fringes of a large town. It could never be truly independent and had to negotiate endless agreements over the provision of gas, use of hospitals and a cemetery, water supply and sewage disposal. In a multitude of ways its fortunes were tied to Birmingham's. There was also a limit to services that could be provided locally. In the 1870s Mr Tipper was already demanding a free library and reading room which the local board, encumbered by debt and ever continuing legal costs, could never hope to finance.[11]

In 1891 Balsall Heath finally succumbed to Birmingham's charms, lured partly by the promise of their own library and swimming baths which still, at the moment, grace Moseley Road today.

Mr James Pass, a member of the board in its last years, wrote his own epitaph on its work and felt that it had achieved a great deal: "...pride was taken in the fact that in place of a suburb containing only a few inhabitants dwelling in scattered cottages, Balsall Heath had now become a populous quarter containing rows of streets and some thirty thousand inhabitants..."[12]

A governing body had seen Balsall Heath through its early difficult phase of development. By 1891, it was not just a city suburb, it was a district with a strong feeling of identity and local pride.

1. & 2. Minutes of Local Board of Health. July 1865.
3. *Everson*. March 1862.
4. Minutes as above. Nov/Dec. 1862.
5. Ibid. April 1865.
6. Ibid. Dec. 1874.
7. Ibid. Mar. 1882.
8. Report of Dr. Ballard. BRL: 97080. 1873.
9. Minutes as above. Jan. 1873.
10. *The Dart*. 1877.
11. *Everson*. Oct. 1872.
12. Articles in *Birmingham Gazette and Express*. Nov. 6, 1908.

Chapter 6

Independence
c.1862 – 1890

Edward Road Police Station Established 1869.

During the 30 years of Balsall Heath's independence, the population trebled. Enormous pressures on housing forced the pace of building to quicken, although there continued to be great variations in size, style and density. At one end of the spectrum were the gracious and elegant abodes which lined Moseley Road and Belgrave Road. In the middle range were respectable and pleasant villas often with gardens, and the smaller lines of terraces which probably comprised the majority of the housing stock. At the other extreme were the back-to-back houses and crowded courts which abounded in Highgate.

41

Rear of Sherbourne Road, 1963.

Rear of 170 Belgrave Road, 1962.

This was a heyday for builders and brickmakers. The land in Balsall Heath yielded plentiful supplies of good clay for bricks and this became a flourishing industry. Ladypool Lane had two brickyards[1] and "mines of clay" were a well-publicised feature of the Edwards estate land. One of the reasons why so many of the local houses had cellars is reputedly because of the valuable clay which lay beneath!

Largest of the brickworks was Harrisons, situated at Vaughton's Hole. This brickyard was bought by an enterprising man called William Charley, who combined the trades of brickmaker and builder to great advantage. He erected the Brighton Hotel in 1875 to cater for the needs of travellers using the newly-opened railway station in Brighton Road and this was followed by a particularly successful business venture in 1876. He bought up Balsall Heath House, the last remnants of the Haden estate, together with "valuable mine of clay" underneath. After demolition, the clay was turned into bricks which he then used to put up on the original site the impressive Belgrave Hotel, nine shops and 55 cottages![2]

The Brighton Hotel, Ladypool Road.
William Charley lived here himself in the 1880s.

There were other notable builders in Balsall Heath too. John Bowen had his building yard in George Street[3] and his initials can still be seen in the decorative brickwork there. He was the builder of Birmingham's splendid Victoria Law Courts in Corporation Street which opened in 1891 and many other fine public buildings, as well as being a noted local benefactor.[4]

John Bowen.

44

Brickwork in George Street showing JB 1882.

There was plenty of work in all the trades associated with building too. The family firm of Bigwoods, for example, was founded in 1878 by W. J. Bigwood, a blacksmith from Wiltshire. He turned his metalworking skills to good advantage and eventually specialised in iron railings, gates and fire-escapes.[5]

Both housing and businesses were encouraged by the improved communication links with Birmingham. The opening of Brighton Road Railway Station in 1875 was a great advance and gave impetus to the development of housing on the east side of the Moseley Road.

Public transport by road was also changing. With the 1870s came the tram, which was pulled along tram lines set into the surface of the road. At first these trams were horse-drawn and had a speed limit of only eight miles per hour! They were supplanted, however, by steam trams in 1885 which were faster but rather unpopular. Complaints were frequently made to the local board of "obnoxious steam", smoke and fumes, as well as noise, smell and "reckless speed". Special regulations were introduced by the board for Sundays – trams had to reduce their speed to three miles per hour when passing places of worship.[6]

Steam Tram on Stratford Road near Ladypool Road, c.1906.

The trams must have made very slow progress around Balsall Heath as by this time small chapels and missions had sprung up all over the district. Moseley Road itself was studded with fine religious buildings. St. Paul's Church was already well established and drawing a large and fashionable congregation. Just up the road rose the impressive twin spires of the Congregational Church, opened in 1862 with seating for a thousand.

The Congregational Church, on the corner of Runcorn Road.

A stone's throw away was the Methodist Church opened in 1872, an offshoot of the Cherry Street Chapel in Birmingham which had been founded in 1782 by John Wesley himself. This church rapidly achieved great success and popularity with its own Sunday school buildings in Lime Grove opening in 1887.[7]

The church buildings were destroyed by bombing in 1940 but have been rebuilt. The foundation stones were laid in 1949 by Miss Minnie Moon, one of the original members of the church and then aged 91.[8] The church has now closed.

Miss Moon laying the foundation stone.

Rebuilt Methodist Church, Moseley Road.

Lenches Trust Almshouses, Conybere Street.

St. Thomas-in-the-Moors' Church.

The Church of England was also flourishing. St. Thomas-in-the Moors in Lincoln Street opened in 1883 and was interesting in its connections with the Cox family. William Sands-Cox donated both land and money for the church to be built in memory of his father, Edward Townsend Cox. Sadly it is no longer there.[9]

Old Saint Alban's Church.

The Pollock brothers.

St. Alban's Church in Highgate had smaller beginnings in a mission established in 1865 by the Pollock brothers. They weathered a serious attack on their high-church rituals in 1867 and went on to stay for 25 years.[10] They were especially remarkable for the quality of their pastoral work in the heavily populated district around the church. A splendid new building was opened in 1881, still a landmark today, together with the charming group of Lenches Trust Almshouses which were erected in 1880.

The church was very well attended, with Sunday schools that had 1,600 children on the register in 1887. Summer excursions were the highlight of the year. On one occasion, 1,189 children together with 210 teachers and a brass band, processed from Leopold Street. to Camp Hill Station to board the excursion trains![11]

Below: 1913 procession.   *Above: St. Albans Church, opened 1881.*

Equally important were the church's day schools, which were founded in 1869 and still serve the community today in newer buildings.

St. Alban's Infant School, 1913.

Meanwhile, the manufacturing industry was establishing itself in Balsall Heath, although mostly on a small scale. Rylands, in Haden Street, was one of the few larger works and still continues today as a family firm with an international reputation for paint and varnish. Its origins were in Ashted in the late-18th century, as suppliers of lacquers – a means of giving metals a fine-coloured glossy finish. The firm's fortunes were dramatically improved by John Llewellyn-Ryland in the mid-19th century. He was a great innovator and said to be the master of a secret process for applying lacquer without heat; a process which he is said to have acquired on his travels to China! The buildings still in use today are those originally purpose built for the firm in 1863.[12]

Rylands Factory,
Haden Street.

Below left: Ryland
workers, c.1914.

Below: A varnish maker
at Rylands, 1911.

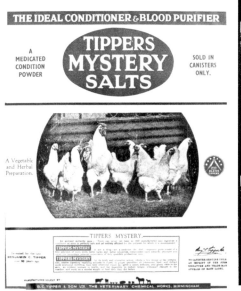

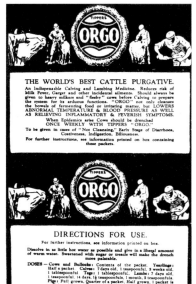

A fine array of adverts gives some idea of the diversity of Tippers' products.

Another interesting factory in Balsall Heath was that of the board member, Benjamin Tipper. He came to Birmingham in 1870, having previously worked in the carpet trade in Kidderminster. He must have had some success in this since he was able to build a fine house called "The Shrubbery" in Tindal Street, behind whose impressive frontage lay his animal food factory.[13]

The firm's products were varied in nature and seem to have included a number of remedies suitable for farm animals. His son joined him in the family business, which continued to trade till 1969.

Both Tippers and Rylands were purpose-built factories but a more usual pattern of individual development in Balsall Heath was for a firm to trace its humble beginnings to a backyard workshop or the front room of a house. Bradbury's of Highgate Square followed this pattern. They trace their origin to 1809 in Highgate, where their premises were originally in the garden of a house. The family wash was accomplished by means of a copper wash tub in the wash house at the back of the house. The story goes that on Mondays, the tub was used for washing

Bradbury's Factory, Highgate Square.

but from Tuesday to Saturday Mr
Bradbury took it over for the
purposes of plating metal! The
firm has always engaged in
producing a versatile array of
metal goods.[14] Perhaps their most
remarkable effort, however, was
for the Birmingham Pageant of
1938, held at Aston to celebrate
the centenary of the city.
Bradbury's made all the armour
for the splendid occasion,
including a special small set worn
by the mascot, who was none
other than a later Mr Bradbury
himself.[15]

An earlier Mr Bradbury.

At the Birmingham Pageant, 1938.

During the 1880s, Highgate and some of the parts of Balsall Heath nearest to Birmingham were developing fast into an area less residential and more industrial in character. Here there was a close intermingling of small workshops and factories, with rather crowded housing.

Ephraim Phillips' factory.

One of the large firms established in this district was Ephraim Phillips in Bissell Street. The original Ephraim Phillips, who purchased premises here for metal manufacture in 1880, was clearly an enterprising character with a flair for new ideas. Two of the machines which he patented were in the Birmingham Museum of Science and Industry: a wire eye forming machine and a thread roller. His proudest and most striking invention, however, was the Duplex Tricycle, first made around 1890. This enabled two people to share the same tricycle, riding side by side. It combined safety with sociability and elegance, allowing the cyclists the benefit of conversation as they rode along. It cost £35 and became very popular. Phillips also made traditionally-shaped bicycles, though it comes as a shock to find that brakes were an optional extra![16]

The Duplex Tricycle.

By the 1880s there was certainly a market for the Phillips bicycles. Hard at work though the population of Balsall Heath undoubtedly was, interest in all kinds of leisure activities was increasing. The Balsall Heath Cycle Club members were pedalling away vigorously together by 1881,[17] to be followed in 1890 by the Apollo Club, based in the Crown Hotel in St. Paul's Road. This had an expensive 4/- subscription and a full programme of time trials, parades and charity sports as well as touring runs.[18] The women put their best feet forward in 1893, too, in founding their own club in Kyrwicks Lane.[19]

Sport in general was a popular form of relaxation, and especially favoured was cricket. The Pickwick Club, now located in Wake Green Road, was founded in 1858, and had its own grounds in St. Paul's Road, as well as a fine reputation. Their most extraordinary moment of glory came in 1878 when they were the only club in Britain to play the Australian touring team, visiting England for the first time. The match was played at Selly Oak, and was remarkable for the imbalance of the teams. Pickwick played 22 against the Australian 11! Unfortunately, rain stopped rather eventful play on the second day of the match.[20]

Australian cricket team, 1878.

Pickwick cricket team, 1878.

Warwickshire v Australia – August 7th 1899.

Cricketers have, of course, been fortunate in the proximity of the Warwickshire County local ground which opened in 1886.

THE SHERBOURNE HOTEL

Is handsomely fitted up with spacious Vaults, Smoke Room, Billiard Room, and accommodation of all descriptions, including Quoit Ground, Arbours, &c., &c.

E. MARTIN'S

SHERBOURNE CONCERT HALL

Has undergone considerable improvement, including a New and Complete Decoration. It is brilliantly lighted, and the accommodation provided by the Stalls, Private and Upper Boxes, and seating in the body of the Hall, is second to none in the district. The entrances and exits are spacious, and the stage is provided with a specially constructed water curtain, as a precaution against fire.

E. MARTIN

Has painted all the Scenery for his Sherbourne Concert Hall.

A GRAND DINNER

Will be held in the Hall on Thursday, October 27th, 1887, at 6 o'clock, prompt.

Tickets, Price 4s., which will include reserved seat for the Opening Night, on Monday, Oct. 31st, 1887, can be obtained from

E. MARTIN,

Sherbourne Hotel,

Balsall Heath.

From The Dart, *1887.*

For sheer variety and ingenuity of entertainment provided in this period, however, there was not much to rival the Sherbourne Hotel. Originally built in Sherbourne Road in 1855, it was apparently a large and commodious establishment. In 1866, 80 gentlemen met here to discuss the Reform Bill in the Assembly Rooms, but there was also an American bowling saloon, billiard room and portrait gallery. Dances were frequent with special omnibus services from Birmingham.[21] To this galaxy of attractions was added another. In 1873, Morris Roberts, an ex prize-fighter, opened his "Birmingham and Midland Zoological Gardens" which lasted for three years against a barrage of furious complaints by local residents.[22] Apparently horses were slaughtered on the premises to cater for the "wild beasts"! A new venture was the roller-skating rinks which replaced the zoo, and which were extremely popular, illuminated by more than 100 lights and accompanied by military bands.[23] These in turn were replaced by Balsall Heath's own music hall from 1887. What a sad loss when the hotel finally closed its doors in 1901!

For many inhabitants, however, more academic leisure pursuits appealed, especially as education became more widely available. There were several private schools in the Balsall Heath area in the 1860s, including one at Stratford House on the Moseley Road and Oakfield

Stratford House School (south aspect), c.1830.

House,[24] but these were expensive and catered for a very small number of pupils.

There were also the two St. Paul's Church schools which provided education for about 400 children between them in the 1860s, but for most children there was nothing but church Sunday schools. However, state education for all was just around the corner.

Under the 1870 Education Act, the King's Norton School Board was set up with responsibility for the education of children who were between the ages of five and ten. It was a daunting task. A report in 1876 established that there was a deficiency of 2,255 places in the whole district, most of which were in Balsall Heath.[25] To meet this need rapidly, the board embarked on an ambitious programme of school building, wisely choosing sites which would allow for further expansion in later years. First of the splendid new schools to open was Mary Street in 1878, with places for 800 children, but such was the rush of applicants in the first week that many had to be turned away.[26] Clifton School, together with new offices for the board, opened later the same year, and Tindal School in 1880. Attendance was not compulsory, even at this stage, however, because there were still insufficient school places.

Clifton Road, Birmingham.

Moseley and Balsall Heath Institute, Moseley Road.

The curriculum taught in the schools was imposed by the central government and concentrated heavily on reading, writing and arithmetic or "The Three Rs" as they were familiarly called. Conditions in the schools were difficult both for staff and pupils. Classes were large, sometimes numbering as many as 70 or 80, and the teaching staff included "pupil-teachers" aged between 13 and 18, who served a form of apprenticeship in the schools. The children learnt to write and do sums on slates, while reading was practised out loud all together. Typically there might be two or three classes going on simultaneously in the school hall, so it is hardly surprising that teachers were often absent with "voice gone" or "teacher's throat".

A crucial event each year was the visit by the government inspector. Under the Payment By Results system, the size of the government grant was determined by individual pupils' average attendance and attainment, so a favourable inspector's report was obviously desirable.

In spite of the difficulties, the board schools undoubtedly had a positive effect on standards of literacy, and there was considerable interest in adult education, reflected in the self-improvement societies which sprang up in Balsall Heath in the 1880s. Some of these were based in the new board schools, while most of them met in various public houses. Best and brightest of these societies was the Moseley and Balsall Heath Institute, originally founded in 1876.

Moseley and Balsall Heath Institute doorway.

The emphasis here was on advanced education, although it had its own vigorous choral and dramatic societies. Earnest fundraising included a huge bazaar in the Town Hall in Birmingham in 1883 which took over £1,400, a truly substantial sum of money in those days. Locally-based attractions did well too. A dramatic entertainment in Clifton School in 1880 drew large audiences every night.

All efforts were crowned in 1883 with the opening of the magnificent Institute building in the Moseley Road, elegantly constructed by the local builder, John Bowen.

The Institute was the cultural focus of both Balsall Heath and Moseley for many years, attracting such nationally famous figures as Charles Dickens and Oscar Wilde.[27]

Such academic pursuits were not to everybody's tastes, however. Many inhabitants had very little leisure time as the working day was long and arduous, and there was little cash to spare. For many, the public house acted as a social focus for every kind of sport and pastime from cockfighting to cards, song and dance. A glimpse of this other world is seen in a magazine report on activities under the Kyrwicks Lane railway arches in 1882. Apparently this rather dark and forbidding area was used by gangs of "roughs" who spent Sundays playing at "pitch and toss" and other games from as early as six in the morning till dusk when "beery pugilists" (boxers) came on the scene to settle their differences.[28]

An alternative had been suggested as early as 1833 by the Select Committee on Parks and Open Spaces. This emphasised the need for open space in towns "reserved for the amusement of the humbler classes... Great complaint is made of drinking houses, dog fights and boxing matches yet unless some opportunity for other recreation is afforded to workmen, they are driven to such pursuits."

Undoubtedly it was this conviction that encouraged both Lord Calthorpe and Miss Ryland to donate parkland to Balsall Heath; Lord Calthorpe in 1857 for Calthorpe Park, and Miss Ryland in 1873 for Cannon Hill Park. In their inaugural messages, both made reference to the desire to promote "healthful recreation" and Lord Calthorpe wanted to restrict the use of the park to walks rather than games, which might be of dubious character.[29] Cannon Hill Park, in particular, was immensely popular with the inhabitants of Balsall Heath, and attracted visitors of every kind to walk or go swimming or boating.

Saturday evening promenaders at one of the park's regular concerts, from The Dart, *1888.*

Lake in Cannon Hill Park,
Birmingham

My time has been very pleasantly
filled in here

1880 ENTRANCE GATE, CALTHORPE PARK.   BIRMINGHAM.

Important to all Wage Earners!

THE PROVIDENT DISPENSARY.
SHERBOURNE ROAD.

WHY JOIN ?—To enable you to get the best medical relief and the purest medicine at the least possible cost.

To avoid going, cap in hand, to beg for Hospital Notes or Dispensary Tickets to Subscribers, who often simply patronise and pauperise those whom they affect to help.

To save the painful difficulty in which a heavy Doctor's Bill plunges a man who has only his weekly wages to count upon.

To pay a penny or so a week is scarcely felt, whereas to pay a big lump sum often cripples a man for years, if not for life.

JOIN, THEN, and show by your example the value of Independence, Self-Help, and Self-Respect.

For full particulars apply at the Dispensary, or to

A. R. TAYLOR, Hon. Sec.

The health of the local inhabitants was also the concern of William Sands Cox, a grandson of Rev. Dr. John Cox of Longmoors, and a prominent Birmingham figure. He founded Queen's College, a medical school, in 1828, and also in 1840 The Queen's Hospital, which closed in 1993. In his will of 1875 he bequeathed money for three dispensaries. One of these was built in Sherbourne Road, Balsall Heath and it provided a self-help scheme for working class people to obtain medicine and medical advice. Thousands of people made use of this institution over the years, until it was superceded by national health provision.[30]

This was the district then, that the city of Birmingham now annexed. It has a strong life of its own, an enterprising and energetic population of great variety. They were to lose their independent status but gain enormous benefit – especially efficient sewerage!

1. *Everson.* 1854 and 1869. Census 1841 and 1871.
2. O.S. Map 1888. *Everson* Jan. 1900. Obituary.
3. Census 1871.
4. *The Dart.* July 1891.
5. Information supplied by Bigwoods of Woodfield Road and St. Paul's Church parish magazine. BRL: 313422.
6. Minutes of Local Board. Nov. 1885.
7. *Moseley Road Methodist Church. The Story of Sixty Years.* 1932. (lent by the church).
8. Centenary booklet. (lent by the church).
9. *Edward Townsend Cox.* BRL; 314413 and Showell's Dictionary of Birmingham.
10. *Vaughton's Hole. 25 Years in it* by J. S. Pollock. 1890.
11. *Father Pollock and His Brother.* Pub. 1912.
12. Information supplied by Rylands, Balsall Heath and *Lacquers* by J. W. Ryland. Pub. 1910.
13. *Birmingham, Moseley and Kings Heath Journal.* 1925 and O.S. Map 1888.
14. Information supplied by the present Mr Bradbury.
15. Programme for the Pageant. 1938.
16. Information from the firm and Birmingham Post. 1974.
17. *The Owl* July 1881.
18. The Apollo Cycling Club: BRL: 385685.
19. *Everson's Directory.* 1896-1901.
20. Pickwick Club Centenary Booklet. 1958. BRL: 661105 and O.S. Map 1888.
21. *Everson.* April and May 1866.
22. Ibid. May 1873 and Local Board Minutes. Dec 1873/Jan 1874.
23. *The Dart.* 1878.
24. Census. 1841 and 1861.
25. Minutes of King's Norton School Board. July 1876.
26. Ibid. April 1878.
27. History of Moseley and B. H. Institute. BRL: 332978.
    and Birmingham Institutions. D49.
    and Programmes. BRL: 243692.
28. *The Dart.* 1882.
29. Inauguration of Calthorpe Park. 1857. BRL: 663184 and obituary notice. Miss Ryland. BRL: 243130.
30. Minute Books and Annual Reports of the Dispensary. BRL: 660819.

Chapter 7

Flourishing Suburb
c.1890 – 1914

After the annexation of 1891, tangible evidence of the city's interest in the area was urgently needed and this was to be supplied by the promised Free Library and Swimming Baths. Balsall Heath Library opened its doors in 1896; a fine and imposing architectural landmark on the Moseley Road, complete with clock tower, and still a symbol of local identity and pride today. Its character has changed, however. In the early years silence prevailed and the assistants fetched books on request from the high bookshelves around the walls!

The Baths and Library, Moseley Road, 1910.

Interior of Library, 1910, with separate tables for ladies and boys, and "No Conversation".

The Baths took longer to complete and the city may well have regretted promising to build them, for they turned out to be extraordinarily expensive. Although the site was acquired in 1894, it was another 13 years before the Baths opened. The difficulty lay in the boring of an artesian well for the water supply, which required an unexpected depth of 727 feet. Building costs also amounted to an amazing £33,000! The opening in 1907 was certainly worth celebrating.[1]

Balsall Heath was delighted, especially as the Baths included not just two swimming pools but also bathrooms and washing facilities as well, a much used and appreciated amenity at that time.

Souvenir programme.

Moseley Road Baths – opened October 30th, 1907.

71

Interior of Moseley Road Baths. The First Class pool.

Although the annexation had passed off smoothly, considerable unpleasantness arose over the transfer of educational responsibility from the King's Norton School Board to the Birmingham School Board. The problem was that the King's Norton Board had raised substantial loans to pay for their building programme, and were planning to repay them over the years out of the rates. Unfortunately for them, the loss of Balsall Heath meant an enormous drop in their income from rates but Birmingham nevertheless insisted that the loans were still the responsibility of the King's Norton Board. This was obviously unfair, but it took a petition to the House of Lords to achieve a compromise agreement and even then King's Norton was left with a hefty bill! To make matters worse, the board now even had to pay rent for the offices which they had built themselves in Clifton Road. This all led to great resentment and bitterness.[2]

Map from Everson's Directory, 1896.

As far as the schools themselves were concerned, however, the change was probably for the better. The Birmingham School Board had a fine reputation, encouraging improvements in teaching methods and a more flexible approach. This was made easier in 1900 when the Government abandoned the system of Payment by Results. The curriculum gradually began to include visits, rambles and lectures, games instead of "Drill" and eventually, swimming in the new Baths.

Dennis Road School (now called Anderton Park). Hand bell drill, 1896.

One major new board school was opened in Dennis Road in 1896, with a much wider range of specialised facilities including its own science and cookery rooms, with a laundry centre added in 1911.

Indian club exercise at Dennis Road School, 1896.

Science class.

Cookery

First aid.

Another development was the establishment of Sherbourne Road Special School. This had its origins in a special class in Moseley Road School in 1896 for children with a variety of difficulties. Here the formal curriculum was adopted sensitively and imaginatively, with an emphasis on art and craft. In 1903 this class moved to Sherbourne Road and became the predecessor of the present Calthorpe School.[3]

The board school on Sherbourne Road also became the centre for school meals provision for needy pupils, from 1906. Soup was offered but not always appreciated. It was served in tin basins and is recalled by most pupils as "absolutely terrible". The children apparently used to tip it down the back of the seats to get rid of it!

A rather more sophisticated educational establishment was the Moseley Road Art School which opened in 1900, for secondary pupils of exceptional artistic talent. It had a high reputation and its elegant building still survives today, though sadly the school itself was closed, in spite of vehement protest, in 1975.

Moseley School of Art.

Meanwhile the population of Balsall Heath continued to grow, from 30,581 in 1891 to 38,827 in 1901,[4] attracted by the opportunities for employment and the availability of inexpensive housing.

This was the period when the last remnants of Balsall Heath's open land finally disappeared. One of the last estates to be developed was that of John Gregory Watkins, who died at his home, Woodfield House, Ombersley, near Worcester, in 1890.

The pattern of development here was quite different to anything yet seen in Balsall Heath. Streets were produced rapidly and mass-produced housing was put up in long terraces, straight on to the streets, as many as 50 at a time, with a second row packed in behind the first.[5]

The Roshven area was also built on this estate land in the 1890s. Here the ambition was again to achieve maximum density of housing to provide quick profit, but the street pattern was much more varied, and interesting decorative detail was added to the houses.

The very last of the open land to go was the site of the present Runcorn Road. This survived as open space till 1905 and even featured a small racecourse which ran in a loop from the railway to Ladypool Lane and back. This was a popular venue for local races, in an era when so many tradespeople had their own horses![6]

Horse buses in Taunton Road, c.1906.

As the population increased there was a growing need for improved transport. Local people had a choice of conveyances: first there were the trains, which ran frequently from Brighton Road and Camp Hill Stations, secondly, there were the horse-drawn omnibuses, with their open topped decks, and thirdly there were the trams.

Buses in Station Street Birmingham, c.1893.

Moseley Road by the New Inn public house.

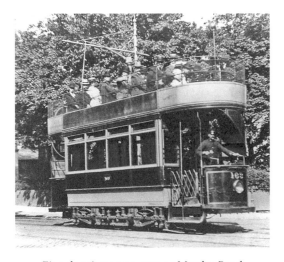

First electric tram to serve on Moseley Road.

Tram routes covered a surprising amount of Balsall Heath, and from 1907 the electric tram replaced the noisy old steam trams.[7] However the final trip at New Year 1907 of the last steam tram, was a nostalgic occasion. Cases of beer were loaded onto the front for the refreshment of the passengers and all along the route people turned out to cheer and collect souvenirs.[8]

The electric tram had its glamorous moments too, however. On special occasions a tram covered with hundreds of coloured bulbs drew the crowds as it made its way along the streets.

Birmingham Illuminated tramcar, Coronation Day, June 22nd 1911.

Balsall Heath was served by two tram depots, one for transport maintenance and training, the other for ambulance repair. The Moseley Road depot was built in 1906, to a design specially suited to this "select and residential area". The second depot opened in Highgate Road in 1913.[9]

Moseley Road tram depot.

Interior of Highgate Road depot.

Moseley Road tram depot staff.

The availability of excellent transport and a large local work force encouraged the development of industry. In the 1890s an astonishing range of goods were manufactured locally, including: artificial teeth, beer and mineral waters, brass bedsteads, candles, coaches, coffins, flags and banners, flint glass, horseshoes, perambulators, watches, wheels, wire and zinc. This was a time when enterprising people flocked into the area, seeking to make their fortunes, and some succeeded. One example is that of Dennis Bailey who grew up in Balsall Heath. On leaving Hope St. School, he borrowed 30 shillings and set himself up as a window cleaner with a bike, bucket and ladder. From these small beginnings he became by 1980, head of the Sheldon Group of industrial cleaning, with a turnover of a million pounds![10]

Balsall Heath also attracted industry which had been established elsewhere. Sames Pianos, for example, was founded in 1855 in central Birmingham, but in 1889 the firm expanded to the cheaper building land in Woodfield Road, constructing a vast four-storey factory with chimney – The Mozart Works![11] Unfortunately, the advantage of being

The building that used to be Sames Piano factory.

SAMES AND SONS
MANUFACTURERS OF
American Organs & Harmoniums,
(BY IMPROVED MACHINERY).
PIANOFORTE WAREHOUSE, EXETER ROW ¿(LATE SUFFOLK STREET),
WORKS, WINDMILL STREET, BIRMINGHAM.
LONDON SHOW ROOMS—97, WIGMORE STREET.   Established 1855.

1882.

close to the railway also caused its downfall. Two large fires were caused by sparks from the trains, setting fire to the wood store. The first fire in 1913 caused extensive damage but the final blow was that of 1923 which destroyed both the roof and the business.[12]

A surprising feature of a number of Balsall Heath firms is that so many, founded in the 1890s, survived for about a hundred years. One such was Camera Bellows, Runcorn Road, who made the flexible bellows parts of cameras. Their work was internationally famous.

An even larger concern was J. H. Butchers, on the Moseley Road, who manufactured transfers of all kinds. It was founded in the 1890s and moved to this site in 1909. The work called for skilled hands and these

The old design room at Butchers, showing the lithographic stones they used.

were found in the ex-pupils of the adjacent Moseley Road School of Art. The firm also had a worldwide reputation, and continues, based in Redditch. The premises are now "The Old Print Works" – a community arts hub.

The Home of Britain's Best Transfers.

THESE WORKS have just been built by us, and specially equipped with the very latest and most up-to-date machinery for producing the most perfect

═══════ T R A N S F E R S. ═══════

Our whole attention is devoted to producing Transfers, and our speciality is

TRANSFERS FOR THE CYCLE AND MOTOR TRADES.

We use only the Finest Colors and Materials, and employ only the Best Labour.

OUR TRANSFERS are therefore the Best, and our prices the Lowest.

Write for Illustrated Price List.

J. H. BUTCHER & CO., 506, Moseley Road, BIRMINGHAM.

(Ten minutes from New Street Station).

From The Cycle and Motor Trader, *1909.*

A number of other businesses too, had their origins in this period. Elcock's, metal spinners of Tindal Street, grew from a back garden workshop in the 1890s till it eventually took over the entire family house and the one next door too. They have now gone and so have Ambler's Funeral Directors which moved to Kings Heath in 1967. This firm was established in Longmore Street in the 1890s, using horse-drawn hearses. They had a team of 34 horses at one time and didn't make the change to motorised vehicles till 1942.[13]

A funeral procession of Ambler's carriages.

85

A scene from the Mullis' yard showing Mr Mullis senior holding one of their ponies while his son sits astride it. The little girl clutching a rabbit is his sister, c.1910.

Moseley Road Fire Station.

Several building firms dated from the 1890s too. Baker's of Woodfield Road started out in the front room of a house in Edward Road. Another local firm now gone was Bendy's, Interior Decorators of Brighton Road.

An interesting service industry run from a back yard was Mullis, Coal Merchants of Edward Road. Here, the premises were purpose built with a double-door entry to the yard and stables behind the house. From here, coal was taken around the streets by horse and cart.

The fire service also continued to operate by horse power at this time. It was not till 1909 that the local fire engines were motorised, spurred on by the opening of a splendid new fire station which opened on the Moseley Road in 1912.[14]

Meanwhile, open space for recreation was becoming desperately short, especially in the region of Ladypool Lane. Balsall Heath Park was opened in 1893 in response to the need on land donated by John Smith-Ryland.

THE NEW PARK AT BALSALL HEATH.
(From a Photo by our own Artist).

The New Park at Balsall Heath, 1894.

Ladypool Lane also became the site of a splendid new church at this time. St. Barnabas opened as a tin hut mission of St. Paul's in 1890, but energetic fundraising enabled the new building to be opened in 1904.[15] The tower was never built but the church was always well attended with a host of activities for local people. Then in 1970, the church was partially rebuilt after a very serious fire.

Parish of Balsall Heath, Birmingham,

Population 35,000.

Building of the New District Church

of

St. Barnabas,

Ladypool Road.

Amount required to complete and furnish Building, exclusive of Tower,

£2,000.

The Congregational Mission Church, opened in Ladypool Road in 1894.
At one time the front part of the building housed a butcher's shop.

The Society of Friends Hall and Institute, on opening, 1899.

Other new churches were established in this period too – the Roman Catholic church in George Street in 1896, the Baptist church in Edward Road in 1900 and the Church of Christ on Moseley Road in 1912. The largest new religious building however, lay at the other end of Balsall Heath on the Moseley Road. This was the amazing Friends Hall and Institute, constructed at the expense of Richard Cadbury, and opened in 1899.

First beginnings of Quaker activity in the area were in 1875 when an adult class began to meet in Montpellier Street, and a Friends crèche and orphanage was also established here.[16]

By 1896, Sunday school attendances were astonishingly high, using board school premises. There were 48 classes with 961 scholars.[17] In addition, there were other clubs of every description for all ages. The new buildings was designed to accommodate all their activity and included a large hall for 2,000, 37 classrooms, a café, and a well-equipped gymnasium. The Institute went from strength to strength.[18] In 1912 total average attendance was 2,730 people, excluding weekday classes and recreational clubs.[19]

Religious festivals were important events in the calendar but there were other special occasions too. Queen Victoria's 60th Jubilee was

The Crèche.

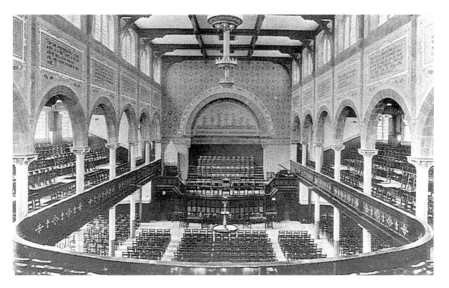

Large Hall.

celebrated in fine style in 1897, and from the Coronation of Edward Vll in 1902 have survived a wealth of photographs and memories. Streets were festooned with flags from end to end. A maypole was erected at the corner of Highgate Road and a whole sheep roasted.

The Café, 1899.

The maypole at Highgate Road, 1902 Coronation celebrations for Edward VII.

Empire Day was celebrated in the local schools from about 1910 to 1918.
Clifton School pupils dressed up for the occasion in national costumes.

Empire Day at Clifton School.

This was Balsall Heath before the First World War. It was an area of
mixed social class, offering opportunities of every kind to its inhabitants.
It was still quite a young community, attracting lively newcomers but with
a strong and vigorous core of longer-term residents. However, world war
lay just ahead.

1. Souvenir of the opening of Moseley Road Baths. BRL: 203599.
2. Minutes of Kings Norton School Board. 1891.
3. Sherbourne Road Special School. Log Books. 1896-1925.
4. V.C.H. Vol 7. Figures derived from census returns.
5. *Everson* 1891 and Minutes of Local Board.
6. *Bygone Birmingham* by Dyke Wilkinson.
7. *A short review of Birmingham Corporation Tramways* by Hardy and Jacques.
8. *Sunday Mercury*. 18-10-36.
9. As 7 above.
10. *Evening Mail*. 14-5-80.
11. Minutes of Local Board. March 1889.
12. *Birmingham Gazette*. 27-8-13 and 30-8-23.
13. Information supplied by Amblers, King's Heath.
14. BRL register of new buildings. 1912.
15. St. Paul's parish magazines. 1890 on.
16. Report and balance sheet for crèche. BRL: 67173.
17. Exec. cttee min bks for Highgate Sunday Afternoon School (from the Friends Meeting House, Moseley Road).
18. *Richard Cadbury* by Helen Alexander.
19. Annual reports. Friends Meeting House.

Ladypool Road Post Office at the junction of Newport Road.

Taylor's gramophone and cycle shop at Taunton House on the corner of Roshven Road.

Chapter 8

Two World Wars
c.1914 – 1945

Mr Stiles' shop, Ladypool Road, 1914.

The First World War came as a terrible shock to Britain and there was a huge surge of patriotic feeling which swept away everything before it. At that time, no one could imagine the horrors of trench warfare which were to come nor the enormous loss of life to be incurred.

A rather bitter story has survived from this time illustrating the depth of antagonism felt for German sympathisers. In 1914 there was a pork butcher's shop in Ladypool Road, which was run by a Mr Stiles. One evening he had rather too much too drink in the Clifton Public House, and unwittingly remarked that he would like to see the Germans win the War. He returned home to find his shop ablaze with its windows smashed. He was forced to give up the business.

Many local people died in the First World War and it was a source of great relief and joy when peace came at last. There was dancing in the streets, and crowds gathered. In Mary Street and Edward Road, one of the pubs rolled out a huge barrel of beer for the street party, and a big bonfire was lit.

Peace party in Ladypool Avenue, 1918.

The period between the two wars is vividly remembered by a lot of people. The physical landscape at this time was mainly unchanging and there was a feeling of stability about the area. It was heavily populated and full of life and activity.

This was a time when a lot of women were full-time housewives, without the benefits of various modern inventions. Housework was a major operation involving a lot of hard labour such as scrubbing and polishing. Washing was similarly demanding. Few houses had running hot water, so first the water had to be heated, the washing done in a "maiding" tub, agitated by hand, with a "dolly-peg". Then it had to be put through a mangle, dried and ironed. Nor were families as small as today's. Often there would be a large number of children, and maybe even grandparents or relatives sharing the house too.

Food preparation was also, therefore, a time-consuming process, and shopping was a matter of either frequent excursions to the shops, since there were no refrigerators or freezers, or buying from barrows in the street. An enormous variety of goods and services were traded in this way: milk from churns, freshly baked bread and cakes, salt cut from large blocks, fish from the market, vegetables, knife sharpening, rag and bone collection and coal delivery.

Philip Fowler, aged 14, delivering the milk.

Shopping areas also developed fast to cater for the needs of the people, especially in Gooch Street, Edward Road and most famous of all, Ladypool Lane. These were the days when butchers sold meat "home-killed" in their own yards, when bakers really baked bread and even medical remedies were handmade. A host of small shops abounded and the atmosphere of Ladypool Lane in particular often resembled a fairground. Saturday night was the climax of the week "Down the Lane". There was excitement in the air as the multitude of butchers' shops auctioned off their meat at bargain prices – sometimes even as late as 11

Mason's shop in Ladypool Lane.

The Jones family's coconut shy at the fairground behind the Olympia Cinema in Ladypool Lane.

o'clock at night. Goods spread out all over the pavement, market stalls lit by naptha flares stood in the roadway and entertainment of every kind was on offer, from buskers and bands to performing monkeys and coconut shies.

Baker's shop in Ladypool Road.

There was a strong sense of local community in the area and Balsall Heath was noted for its friendliness and neighbourly goodwill. Freda Cox, who was, at one time, the landlady of the New Inn public house on the Moseley Road, recalls collecting for charity, "Balsall Heath folk had hearts as big as buckets."

The years between the wars were hard times for a lot of people, however. Employment was scarce and it's interesting to find that the Brighton Road railway bridge was widened in 1923 under a scheme for the unemployed.[1]

Percy Shurmer was a local councillor at the time, and also lived in the area, in Belgrave Road. He stood out as a campaigner for the welfare of the local people, organising many clubs and activities including a jazz band. He was regarded as a local hero.

Brighton Road, bridge widening.

At the Luxor, Mr Baker is seated fourth from the left.

Pringle's Palace (later called the Triangle).

Meanwhile, important changes were taking place along the Moseley Road. From 1916, the daring new motor buses made their appearance and in spite of everyone's initial doubts, proved themselves as rivals to the electric trams or "boneshakers".[2] As Birmingham's suburbs stretched further outwards, petrol power was a cheaper alternative than laying expensive new tram lines. The last tram in Birmingham made its final run in 1953 and local people remember the crowds that gathered to wish it farewell. Some placed pennies on the rails which the tram obligingly squashed flat, providing novel keepsakes!

The motor bus was not the only modern invention to come to the district; there was also the cinema. First on the scene in Balsall Heath was Pringle's Palace, in Gooch Street later known as the Triangle, and this was quickly followed by five others within the next two years.[3] The films were, of course, silent but accompanied by live music which varied from a single pianist to a large orchestra. One cinema band which played at the Luxor, in Balsall Heath Road, is well recalled by Mr Baker, a local businessman.

Programme for the Balsall Heath Picture House, c.1914 (later called the Luxor).

Left: 1914.   Above: Mr George Harris.

Styles and pretensions varied enormously among the cinemas. The Imperial on Moseley Road, for example, was a rather select and dignified place, showing better films and charging higher prices than elsewhere. By contrast, the Olympia on Ladypool Road was very small and always very crowded. Saturday afternoon here was the "penny rush" show for children, with a new episode of the serial every week, always finishing with a thrilling cliff-hanger. Since the children's behaviour was often very noisy and lively, the usherettes were equipped with canes which were often put to good use!

Please Patronise Advertisers.

OLYMPIA PICTURE THEATRE,

Ladypool Road.

General Manager : - - Mr. FRANCIS E FORRESTER.

Continuous Performance.

Every Evening from 6-30, Saturdays 6 o'clock

Matinees : ¯Monday & Wednesday at 3.

Good, Clean, Moral Pictures only.

The Latest and Best.

Prices of Admission :-

Matinees, 2½, 4d. & 6. Evenings, 4d., 5d. & 7d.,

Telephone. Victoria 124. including Amusement Tax

The Hall is now thoroughly Heated and Ventilated.

Olympia Cinema.

The Carlton.

The Carlton Cinema in Taunton Road, was a later arrival in 1930. It was exceedingly luxurious with a passenger lift to all the balcony seats, and an organ which rose up automatically in the middle of the auditorium.

The great new excitement in 1929 was "the Talkies". Many leaders of the film industry thought that these would never catch on, but indeed the new talking pictures were an immediate and amazing success, though bitterly attacked by the cinema musicians! The Olympia in Ladypool Road until recently boasted its new films in lettering on the front of the building, "Talkies".

By the end of the 1930s Balsall Heath was, in many ways, a good place to live. Some of the housing was cramped and there was too little open space, but there were good schools, swimming baths and a library. There were excellent shopping streets, lots of entertainment and good transport to Birmingham itself. People remember Balsall Heath as it was then with affection and pride.

The Second World War came as a great blow and left the area seriously damaged.

* * *

On the declaration of war in 1939, immediate precautions were taken for fear of bomb and gas attacks. Gas masks were issued to everyone and a hasty scheme was drawn up for the evacuation of school-aged city children. This was a heartbreaking enterprise. Imagine the agonising decisions parents had to take, whether to keep their children with them to face all the risks of bombing, or to send them off on their own, to a completely unknown family in strange surroundings. For many, the decision was evacuation. As early as August 1939, a party of 56 children and 16 adults, mostly teachers, went off from Highgate Street School to the evacuation centre at Gloucester.[4] Clifton School was also quick off the mark with evacuation plans, and a pitiful list of requirements for the child to take was headed by the gas mask! The expected bombings did not happen immediately, however, and most of the children had returned by Christmas.

Meanwhile in the autumn of 1939, Balsall Heath grimly prepared for war. Many houses had Anderson shelters in their gardens, but these were not very satisfactory as they were damp at the best of times and at worst, completely flooded with water. Some people retreated into indoor shelters in cellars while courts of houses tended to have a communal shelter in the courtyard. For many though, the safest place was the public shelter and there were a number of these in Balsall Heath. One was under Sames Piano factory in Woodfield Road, another under Moseley Road Congregational Church, one under a shop at one end of St. Paul's Road, some in local schools and churches and two were under the St. Paul's Road and Brighton Road railway bridges. Many people also went to relatives in the country or outer suburbs each night, returning home in the morning.

With the approach of enemy bombers, sirens were sounded from the police stations and local factories. At the height of the raids in the autumn of 1940, most working people barely had time to get home from work and have an evening meal before the sirens sounded for the nightly attack.

The first bombs began to fall on Balsall Heath in October 1940. On the same night, Tindal Street School was hit, where people had gone for shelter, and Moseley Road Methodist Church was completely burnt out. November 1940 saw the beginning of the worst period of bombing and the night of November 19th was a black one for Birmingham and for Balsall Heath. In the area between Moseley Road and Pershore Road, for example, no less than 10 bombs fell, and of course the vicinity of the railway line was attacked too. This was the night the Carlton Cinema in Taunton Road was wrecked while it was showing films to a crowded audience.

Moseley Road had, meanwhile, earned the nickname "Bomb Alley". The tram line was hit between Edward Road and Belgrave Road, leaving the rail itself sticking straight up in the air with two trams trapped either side of it. Travelling by tram came to involve getting off at the Edward Road halt and walking to Camp Hill.

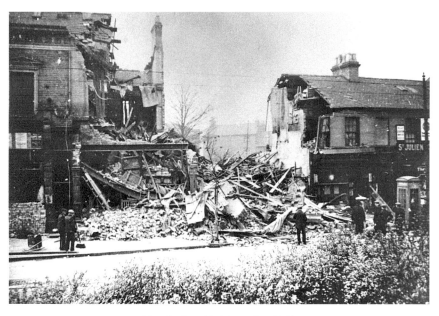

Moseley Road in November 1940.

Gooch Street bomb damage.

Industry in Balsall Heath did not suffer as badly as might have been expected. There were very few really large factories to provide targets for the bombers, and many of the small Balsall Heath workshops and businesses were reserved occupations. Many of the local building firms found they had a huge increase in work. Bakers of Woodfield Road, for example, got a lot of war damage commissions for repair work, and a loft on their premises was commandeered for munitions work. Edwards, in Hertford Street, was an auxiliary fire station. Devey's, the decorating firm in Clifton Road, was at that time also the family home and Mr

*Runcorn Road, looking from the Moseley Road end
and showing some of the Brighton Road Station buildings.*

Mary Street Schools after bombing.

Harbury Road Air Raid Wardens – E Division, c.1943.

Devey remembers an amusing incident. One night an incendiary bomb fell on the roof and his father quickly fetched out one of his long ladders for a bit of do-it-yourself bomb removal. He was, fortunately, successful, except that he got trapped on the roof by an officious air raid warden who came along and removed the ladder!

Meanwhile, ordinary life was no bed of roses. Rationing meant that everyone had a fair share of the food available – but it also meant endless queuing outside shops which invariably ran out of supplies just as you reached the head of the queue. Sunday joints were definitely out – unless you saved your entire meat ration for the week, and special occasions were a nightmare of scrimping and saving for weeks beforehand.

The end of the war produced a massive national celebration in Balsall Heath, street parties were held everywhere and people decorated their houses with bunting and flags. Of course, the scars of war were still there, but at least the fighting was over.

1. *Moseley and King's Heath Journal.* Feb. 1923.
2. *A Short Review of Tramways*, as above.
3. BRL. Register of New Buildings. 1913-15.
4. Upper Highgate School. Log Books.

Chapter 9
Finally – A New Beginning

The years following 1945 were probably the worst there had ever been. For Balsall Heath the fabric of the area had been extensively damaged and it took years to recover from this. The decrease in the number of houses could have been an asset, providing more open space for the crowded population, but bomb "pecks" or sites were inadequately cleared and instead became rubbish dumps and playgrounds for the next generation. As conditions deteriorated, the cheap housing attracted many of the poorest families in Birmingham, who were then unable to find local employment. It was a long-term disaster.

Balsall Heath today is vastly different. The housing stock has been greatly improved by a programme of urban renewal launched in the 1970s, and by the praiseworthy efforts of housing associations. Open land left by the bombing has at last been cleared and put to good use, while whole new parks have been created such as Pickwick Park in St. Paul's Road and Seven Streets Park in Clifton Road. Much of the old Balsall Heath has regrettably been demolished rather than restored, but there is a lot of new housing thanks to both the city and housing associations. The population is full of vigour and determination.

In some ways, Balsall Heath today strongly resembles that of a hundred years ago. This was a time when newcomers flocked to Balsall Heath to join families and friends already there, and to make a living for themselves. The last 10-20 years have seen a similar influx of newcomers to Balsall Heath from different parts of the world, but especially from the Caribbean and Asia. These people have enormously enriched the traditional cultural patterns of the area, and today it is a model of a thriving inner-city community.

Religious life is also flourishing. The old St. Paul's Church has gone but has moved to an exciting Church Centre in Edward Road, together with the Church of Christ. Here, provision is made for elderly people as well as other local groups during the week. New religions have come too. Balsall Heath now boasts several Sikh temples, and a number of mosques –

St Paul's Church on the move.

*Celebration time at the dedication of the new Church Centre in Edward Road.
Home to both St. Paul's Church and the Church of Christ.*

Refurbished shops in Ladypool Lane.

Nelson Mandela School. An award-winning design.

The Birmingham Central Mosque in Belgrave Road

The new Lane Medical Centre in Stoney Lane.

New housing.

Old housing restored.

Balsall Heath Carnival and Fun Run, 1991.

*Carnival 1984,
Sinclair Spectrum.*

gracious new buildings which have involved a large amount of pulling together by much of the local community. A new school has opened too – the Nelson Mandela School, and there is a push for new business enterprises as well. Community commitment is high and Balsall Heath Carnival was ranked as one of the best in Birmingham though no longer continuing.

It was the centenary of the annexation to Birmingham in 1991. Balsall Heathans might still regret their loss of independence, but they have retained a strong tradition of collective identity and local pride.

Carnival 1989, History Society Float.

117

Balsall Heath – Timeline

1700-1800	Birmingham's population increased. 15,000 to 70,000.
1740s	Establishment of a tannery – site of present Lime Grove.
1767	Alcester Road Turnpike Trust opened a road across Balsall Heath as part of route from country to Birmingham.
1774	Enclosure. The land divided between a small number of people.
1778	Establishment of The Association for the Prosecution of Felons (local inhabitants watch group).
1791	Birmingham Riots – burnt down house of Joseph Priestley in Larches Green, and a school on the Moseley Road.
1829	First of the big estates sold off for development of terrace housing. (Frowd and Moore Estate, Balsall Heath Road and area, including a bridge over River Rea).
1833	Edwards Estate begins to be sold and developed (Edward Road and area).
1840	Opening of London-Gloucester Railway, through Balsall Heath and Camp Hill Station on Moseley Road (near Highgate Road traffic lights).
1846	Horse-drawn omnibus route along the Moseley Road (till 1870s)
1862	Establishment of the Balsall Heath Local Board of Health. (Balsall Heath up till now was administered as part of King's Norton Parish. Under the board it enjoyed independence till 1891). Great improvements in paving of streets, lighting, refuse collection, water supply and – eventually – sewerage (1882). Rapid development of housing and some industry, mainly on west side of Moseley Road.
1872-3	Typhoid epidemic in Balsall Heath and Moseley.
1870s	Horse-drawn trams begin to run.
1873	Opening of Cannon Hill Park.
1885	Opening of Brighton Road Railway Station.
1878	First board school opened – Mary Street followed by Clifton, Tindal, Sherbourne Road.
1891	Balsall Heath annexed to City of Birmingham.
1896	Balsall Heath Library opened.
1907	Moseley Road Baths in Balsall Heath opened.
1912	First cinemas in Balsall Heath open. The Triangle in Gooch Street and Moseley Road Picture Palace.
1940-45	Extensive bomb damage during 2nd World War.

Balsall Heath Population Figures

1865	Approx	10,000 (Estimated by the local Board of Health)
1871	Census	13,615
1875	(Local board)	20,632
1881	Census	22,734
1911	Census	39,218

Main Source Material

1. *Everson's Chronological History of Balsall Heath, King's Heath and Moseley*. 13 vols.

2. *Aris's Gazette.*

3. Maps and Plans relating to Balsall Heath including Title Map, Estate plans and Ordnance Survey from 1888.

4. Minute Books of the Balsall Heath Local Board of Health.

5. *The Dart* and *The Owl.*

6. Minutes of the King's Norton School Board, and individual school log books.

7. Census material 1841 – 81.

8. Dircctorics including *Wrightson's Directory* 1847, and *Everson's Directory* 1896 – 1901.

9. Church records including parish magazines, minute books, accounts etc.

10. Register of new buildings 1913 – 16.

11. Lee Crowder, Collection of Deeds.

12. BRL Collection of newspaper cuttings, including Bickley.

13. Records and information supplied by local businesses.

14. Annual reports and programmes. Moseley and Balsall Health Institute.

15. Minute Books and Annual Reports. Sherbourne Road Provident Dispensary.

16. *Faces and Places* magazines.

17. Souvenir of opening of Moseley Road Baths. 1907.

18. Cinema programmes. 1913 – 16.

Index